MAILBOX®

High-Frequ... Word Booklets

MW00379148

1

16 Booklets for Emergent and Beginning Readers

- **Provides Practice With Reading High-Frequency Words**

- **Improves Fluency**

- **Builds Comprehension**

- **Motivates Students to Read**

Managing Editor: Allison E. Ward

Editorial Team: Becky S. Andrews, Kimberley Bruck, Karen P. Shelton, Diane Badden, Thad H. McLaurin, Sharon Murphy, Kimberly Brugger-Murphy, Karen A. Brudnak, Sarah Hamblet, Hope Rodgers, Dorothy C. McKinney, Ada Goren

Production Team: Lisa K. Pitts, Pam Crane, Rebecca Saunders, Jennifer Tipton Cappoen, Chris Curry, Sarah Foreman, Theresa Lewis Goode, Ivy L. Koonce, Clint Moore, Greg D. Rieves, Barry Slate, Donna K. Teal, Tazmen Carlisle, Amy Kirtley-Hill, Kristy Parton, Cathy Edwards Simrell, Lynette Dickerson, Mark Rainey

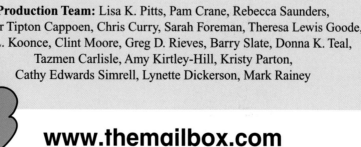

www.themailbox.com

©2005 The Mailbox®
All rights reserved.
ISBN10 #1-56234-650-4 • ISBN13 #978-156234-650-8

Manufactured in the United States
10 9 8 7 6 5 4 3 2

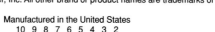

Table of Contents

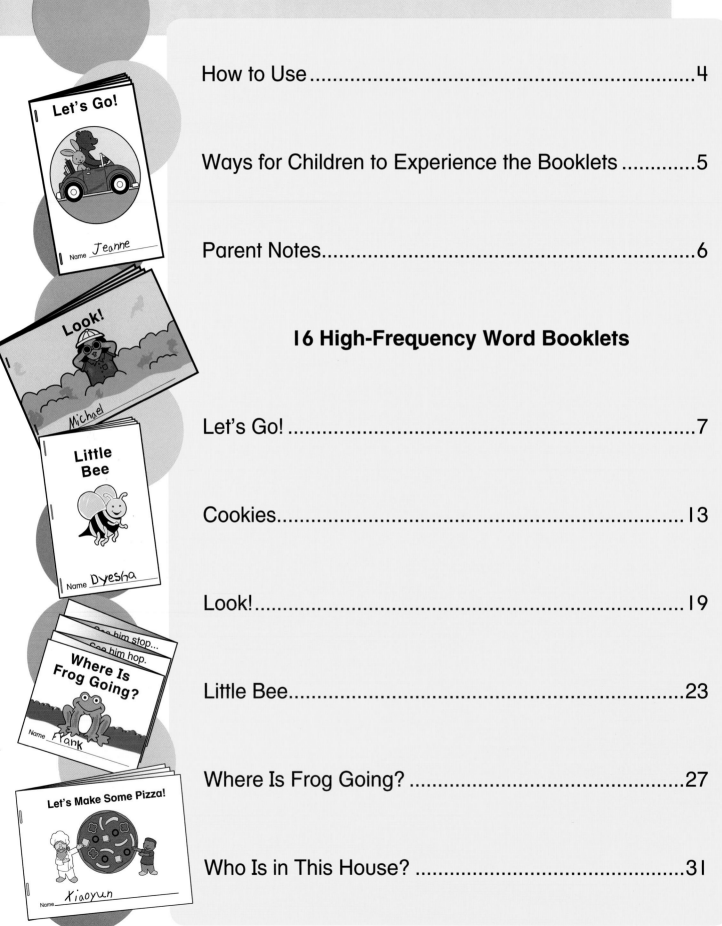

How to Use

Everything you need to successfully make and use the high-frequency word booklets with your students can be found right on the teacher page that accompanies each booklet.

Teacher Page

Materials list and directions for making the booklet

Completed booklet

Who Is in This House?

Booklet Materials:

copy of pages 32–34 for each student
crayons
scissors
glue
stapler

Making the booklet:

1. Have the student color the cover and booklet pages.
2. Cut out the door patterns on page 34.
3. Glue a door to each booklet page. Allow time for the glue to dry.
4. Cut out the cover and booklet pages.
5. Stack the pages in order behind the cover; then staple them together along the left-hand side.
6. Have the student write his name on the booklet cover.

Activity for introducing the featured high-frequency words before reading the booklet

Introducing the featured words:

Introduce the words listed by writing them on the board and discussing them. Or, if desired, introduce the words with the help of this drawing activity! Post a sheet of chart paper in your large-group area. Write each listed word on a separate index card. Present a card to youngsters and then help them identify the word. Draw a large square on the chart paper. Show youngsters each remaining card one at a time, and as they identify the word, add a different element to the square to transform it into a house. You may wish to add items such as a door, two windows, a chimney, curtains, and a porch. Have students identify the finished drawing. Then explain that the book you're about to share is about several houses and their interesting occupants!

Building fluency:

Meow! Woof! Tweet! Youngsters jazz up rereadings of the booklet with sound effects! After students have read the booklet several times, ask them to name the sound each animal makes. Then, during subsequent rereadings, invite them to make the appropriate sound after reading the text inside each door.

Featured
High-Frequency Words

who	house
is	a
in	little
this	

31

How to use the booklet to build fluency

High-frequency words featured in the booklet

Ways for Children to Experience the Booklets

- **Teacher Models**—Read a booklet with the students while they follow along in their own copies; then have students reread the booklet on their own.

- **Close the Book and Listen**—Have everyone close his or her booklet and listen as you read. This helps students focus on how the reading sounds.

- **Choral Reading**—Have a group of students read the booklet aloud together after you've read it with them following along.

- **Echo Reading**—Read a page with expression; then have the students chorally reread the page.

- **Paired Reading**—Pair students; then have each child take turns reading his booklet to his partner.

- **Performance Reading**—Have a student take on the voice, attitudes, stance, and personality of a character in the booklet.

- **Readers' Theater**—Have a student (or a group of students) read a booklet aloud while acting it out.

- **Home Reading**—Send booklets home for students to read with a parent or other adult.

- **Shared Book Reading**—Make a big-book version of the booklet. Discuss the title, cover art, and illustrations. Read and reread the big book several times with students.

Look, look!
I can read this book!

Ask me to read it with you.

Look, look!
I can read this book!

Ask me to read it with you.

Note to the teacher: Duplicate a note for each child. Send the note home with a booklet when appropriate.

Let's Go!

Booklet Materials:

copy of pages 8–11 and the booklet
   page on page 12 for each student
crayons
scissors
glue
stapler

Making the booklet:

1. Cut out the cover and booklet
   pages.
2. Stack the booklet pages in order
   behind the cover; then staple them
   together along the left-hand side.
3. Have the student write his name on
   the cover.
4. Have him color the pictures on the
   cover and booklet pages.

Introducing the featured words:

Introduce the words listed by writing them on the board and
discussing them. Or, if desired, pack in some fun by using a suitcase to introduce the words! To do this, write the featured high-
frequency words on separate index cards. Then put all the cards
in a small suitcase or overnight bag. Show youngsters the bag
and ask a volunteer to remove a card from the suitcase. Help
him identify the word; then display it for the class. Continue in
this manner with different students until all the words have been
identified. Then enjoy the booklet together.

Building fluency:

When students have read through the booklet several times,
get them on the right track with these vehicle pointers! Give
each child a copy of a vehicle pattern on page 12. Have each
child color his pattern; then help him glue the cutout vertically
to a craft stick to make a pointer as shown. Have him reread the
booklet, using the vehicle pointer to travel across the pages!

Featured
High-Frequency Words

go	out
up	over
down	and
in	

Let's go

1

Let's Go!

Name _____

3

down,

2

up,

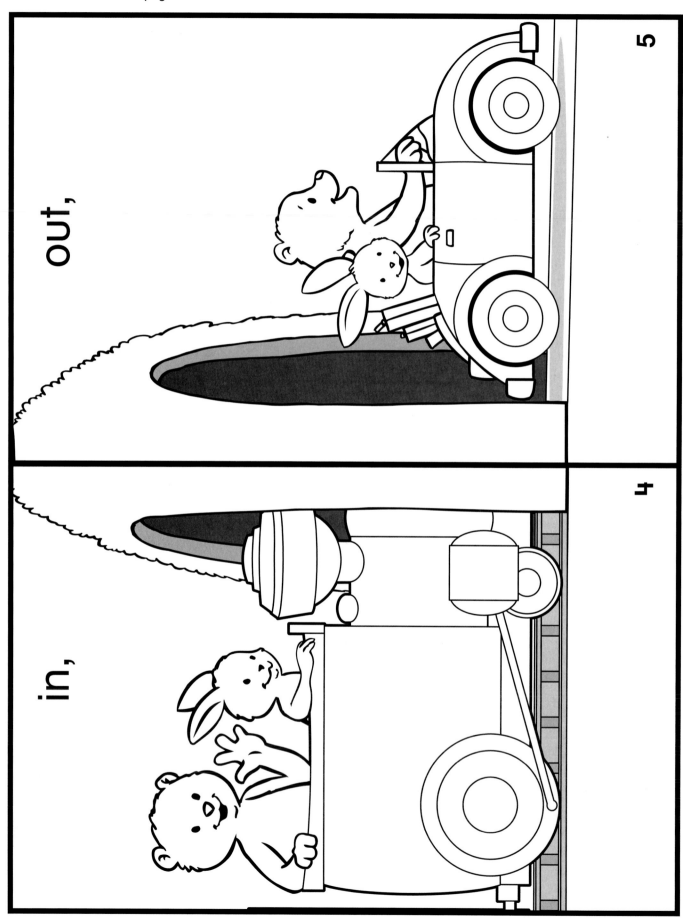

out,

5

in,

4

under,

7

over,

6

Booklet Page 8
Use with "Let's Go!" on page 7.

Vehicle Patterns
Use with "Building Fluency" on page 7.

Cookies

Booklet Materials:

copy of pages 14–17 and the booklet page
   on page 18 for each student
crayons
scissors
stapler

Making the booklet:

1. Cut out the cover and booklet pages.
2. Stack the booklet pages in order behind the cover; then staple them together along the left-hand side.
3. Have the student write her name on the cover.
4. Have her color the pictures on the cover and booklet pages.
5. Have her draw her face on pages 4 and 8.

Introducing the featured words:

Introduce the words listed by writing them on the board and discussing them. Or, if desired, use this activity, which is guaranteed to make your little ones flip! Copy the cookie patterns at the bottom of page 18 onto tagboard and cut them out. Program the back of each cookie with a different featured high-frequency word. Then place all the cookies on a baking sheet (word side down). Offer a child a spatula and have her flip over a cookie. Help her identify the word and then display it for the class. Continue in this manner with different students until all the words have been identified. Then enjoy the booklet together.

Building fluency:

When students have read through the booklet several times, use miniature cookies to inspire even more enthusiastic reading! Give each child three pieces of Cookie Crisp cereal. As she reads the number words on pages 1–3, have her count the pieces and place them on the page. Then have her finish reading the booklet, eating the cookies as she reads each number word.

Featured
High-Frequency Words

one	me
two	I
all	am
for	

Cookies

Name _____

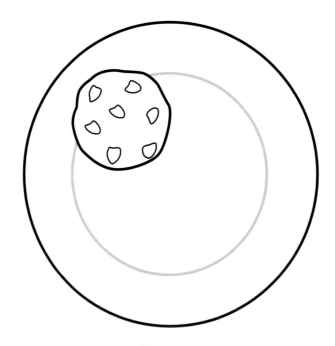

One.

1

Two.

2

Three.

3

All for me!

4

Three.

5

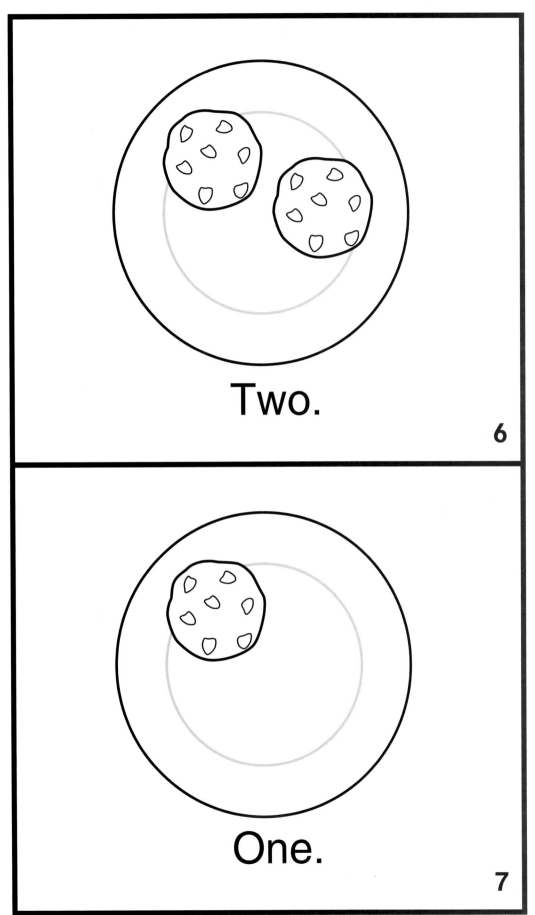

Two.

6

One.

7

Booklet Page 8
Use with "Cookies" on page 13.

I am done!

8

Cookie Patterns
Use with "Introducing the Featured Words" on page 13.

Look!

Booklet Materials:

copy of pages 20–22 for each student
crayons
scissors
stapler

Making the booklet:

1. Cut out the cover and booklet pages.
2. Stack the booklet pages in order behind the cover; then staple them together along the left-hand side.
3. Have the student write his name on the cover.
4. Have him color the pictures on the cover and booklet pages.

Introducing the featured words:

Introduce the words listed by writing them on the board and discussing them. Or, if desired, send your students on a high-frequency word safari! To do this, write each featured high-frequency word on a separate index card. On the back of each card, affix a different animal sticker. Place the cards (animal side out) in a pocket chart. Have a student volunteer name an animal. Flip over that card and help him identify the word. Continue in this manner with different students until all the words have been identified. Then enjoy the booklet together.

Building fluency:

When students have read through the booklet several times, add to the fun with some simple homemade binoculars! For each child, staple together two 1¼" sections of paper towel tube to resemble binoculars. Next, pair students. Have one student in each twosome look through his binoculars at the booklet pictures as his partner rereads the booklet aloud. Then invite the partners to switch roles.

Featured
High-Frequency Words

look	all
I	at
see	the
them	

Look!

Name _____

Look!

1

I see monkeys too.

4

I see them all at the zoo!

ZOO

5

Little Bee

Booklet Materials:

copy of pages 24–25 and the booklet
  page on page 26 for each student
crayons
scissors
stapler

Making the booklet:

1. Cut out the cover and booklet
   pages.
2. Stack the booklet pages in order
   behind the cover; then staple
   them together along the left-hand
   side.
3. Have the student write her name
   on the cover.
4. Have her color the pictures on the
   cover and booklet pages.
5. Instruct her to draw her self-portrait
   on the final page.

Introducing the featured words:

Introduce the words listed by writing them on the board
and discussing them. Or, if desired, introduce the words with
this adorable bee pointer! Color and cut out a copy of the bee
pattern on page 26. Laminate the cutout for durability. Then
tape it to the end of a pointer or yardstick. Write the high-
frequency words from the list on a sheet of chart paper. Then
"fly" the bee pointer from word to word, encouraging students to
help you identify the word each time the bee lands!

Building fluency:

There's sure to be quite a buzz about this unique rereading
of the booklet! When youngsters are comfortable reading the
booklet, encourage them to think about the kind of voice a little
bee would have if it could talk. Then prompt students to use their
littlest voices to read the booklet aloud. If desired, reward youngsters with a snack of honey on crackers!

Featured

High-Frequency Words

a	made
little	for
in	me

1

A little bee

Little
Bee

Name _____

©The Mailbox® • High-Frequency Word Booklets • TEC60912

3

made a little honey

2

in a little tree

Booklet Page 4

Use with "Little Bee" on page 23.

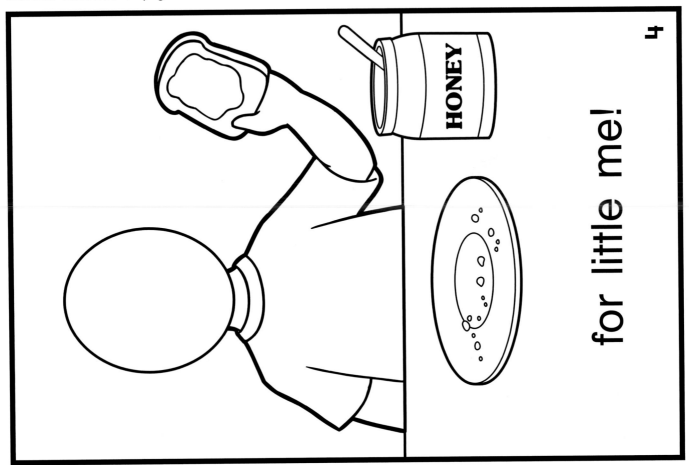

for little me!

4

Bee Pattern

Use with "Introducing the Featured Words" on page 23.

Where Is Frog Going?

Booklet Materials:
copy of pages 28–30
   for each student
crayons
scissors
glue

Making the booklet:
1. Cut out the cover and booklet pages.
2. Glue the cover and booklet pages together as indicated.
3. When the glue is dry, accordion-fold the booklet so that the cover appears on top.
4. Have the student write his name on the cover.
5. Have him color the pictures on the cover and booklet pages.

Introducing the featured words:
   Introduce the words listed by writing them on a board and discussing them. Or, if desired, introduce the words with a froggy flair! To do this, display lily pad cutouts that you have prepared with the high-frequency words. Have each child put a frog sticker on his index finger and take a turn pretending to have the frog hop from one lily pad to another. Help him identify a word and then affix his sticker to the lily pad. After every child has had a turn to identify one or more words, enjoy the booklet together.

Building fluency:
   When students have read through the booklet several times, add to the fun with some hoppin' frog pointers! For each child, affix a small frog sticker or cutout to the end of a craft stick. Have each child run the pointer under the words as everyone reads the booklet in unison. Or have her pretend to have the frog hop from word to word.

Featured
High-Frequency Words

where	is
going	see
him	go
to	his

Where Is Frog Going?

Name _____

See him go.

I

See him hop.

Glue to the back of page 3.

2

See him swim.

Glue to the back of page 4.

3

Who Is in This House?

Booklet Materials:

copy of pages 32–34 for each student
crayons
scissors
glue
stapler

Making the booklet:

1. Have the student color the cover and booklet pages.
2. Cut out the door patterns on page 34.
3. Glue a door to each booklet page. Allow time for the glue to dry.
4. Cut out the cover and booklet pages.
5. Stack the pages in order behind the cover; then staple them together along the left-hand side.
6. Have the student write his name on the booklet cover.

Introducing the featured words:

Introduce the words listed by writing them on the board and discussing them. Or, if desired, introduce the words with the help of this drawing activity! Post a sheet of chart paper in your large-group area. Write each listed word on a separate index card. Present a card to youngsters and then help them identify the word. Draw a large square on the chart paper. Show youngsters each remaining card one at a time, and as they identify the word, add a different element to the square to transform it into a house. You may wish to add items such as a door, two windows, a chimney, curtains, and a porch. Have students identify the finished drawing. Then explain that the book you're about to share is about several houses and their interesting occupants!

Building fluency:

Meow! Woof! Tweet! Youngsters jazz up rereadings of the booklet with sound effects! After students have read the booklet several times, ask them to name the sound each animal makes. Then, during subsequent rereadings, invite them to make the appropriate sound after reading the text inside each door.

Featured

High-Frequency Words

who	house
is	a
in	little
this	

Who Is in This House?

Name _____

Who is in this house?

A cat.

Glue here.

1

Who is in this house?

Glue here.

A dog.

2

Who is in this house?

Glue here.

A bird.

3

Booklet Page 4 and Door Patterns

Use with "Who Is in This House?" on page 31.

Who is in this house?

Glue here.

A little mouse.

4

Let's Make Some Pizza!

Booklet Materials:

copy of pages 36–42 for each student
crayons
scissors
stapler

Making the booklet:

1. Cut out the cover and booklet pages.
2. Stack the booklet pages in order behind the cover; then staple them together along the left-hand side.
3. Have the student write his name on the cover.
4. Have him color the pictures on the cover and booklet pages.

Introducing the booklet:

Introduce the words listed by writing them on the board and discussing them. Or, if desired, introduce the words and the booklet's theme with a pizza presentation! To do this, write each word on a separate red paper circle to resemble a pepperoni slice. Then place the circles in a clean, empty pizza box. Have a child reach into the box and choose a circle. Help him identify the word and then display it for the class. Continue in this manner with different students until all the words have been identified. Then enjoy the booklet together.

Building fluency:

When students have read through the booklet several times, try some playful choral reading to encourage further practice! Play the part of the chef in the booklet. Have the class read each page chorally. Repeat each ingredient as students name it and pretend to put it on a pizza. When the class reads the last page, excitedly say, "Jam!" and pretend to spread jam on the pizza. Have the class shout, "No!" to discourage you from ruining the pretend pizza.

Featured
High-Frequency Words

make	you
some	but
it	do
with	not
if	

Let's Make Some Pizza!

Name _____

©The Mailbox® • High-Frequency Word Booklets • TEC60912

—

Make it with sauce.

2

Make it with cheese.

Booklet Page 3
Use with "Let's Make Some Pizza!" on page 35.

3

Make it with peppers, if you please.

Make it with olives.

4

5

Make it with ham.

But please do not make it with jam!

6

What Do You Like to Eat?

Booklet Materials:

tan construction paper copy of page 44 for each student
copy of pages 45 and 46 for each student
crayons
scissors
stapler

Making the booklet:

1. Cut out the backing and booklet pages.
2. Stack the booklet pages in order; then staple them to the backing where indicated.
3. Have the student write her name on the backing.
4. Have her color the pictures on the booklet pages.
5. After introducing the featured words, help her check the appropriate box on each booklet page.
6. Help her write and draw her favorite food in the box on the backing.

Introducing the featured words:

Introduce the words listed by writing them on the board and discussing them. Or, if desired, introduce the words with added flavor! Write each word on a separate index card. Then place the cards in a small paper lunch bag. Have a child reach into the bag and choose a card. Help her identify the word; then display it for the class. Continue in this manner with different students until all the words have been identified. Then enjoy the booklet together.

Building fluency:

When students have read through the booklet several times, pair them up for a question-and-answer session! Have one child read as his partner follows along in his own booklet and answers the questions. Then have the twosome switch roles.

Featured
High-Frequency Words

what	like
do	to
you	I

Booklet Backing

Use with "What Do You Like to Eat?" on page 43.

What Do You Like to Eat?

Name _____

I really like
to eat

_____.

1

Do you like

carrots?

☐ yes ☐ no

2

Do you like

cake?

☐ yes ☐ no

3

Do you like

noodles?

☐ yes ☐ no

4

Do you like

steak?

☐ yes ☐ no

5

Do you like

apples?

☐ yes ☐ no

6

Do you like

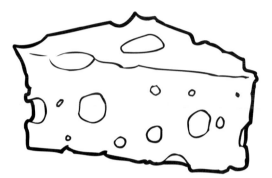

cheese?

☐ yes ☐ no

7

Do you like

oranges?

☐ yes ☐ no

8

Do you like

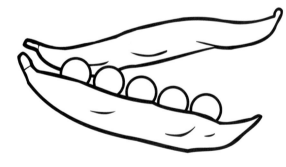

peas?

☐ yes ☐ no

Drew and Sue

He is sleepy. She is not.

2

Booklet Materials:

copy of pages 48–52 for each student
crayons
scissors
stapler

Making the booklet:

1. Cut out the cover and booklet pages.
2. Stack the booklet pages in order behind the cover; then staple them together along the left-hand side.
3. Have the student write his name on the cover.
4. Have him color the pictures on the cover and booklet pages.

Introducing the featured words:

Introduce the words listed by writing them on the board and discussing them. Or, if desired, introduce students to the words with the following fun activity! Write each word listed on a separate index card. Obtain a boy puppet and a girl puppet. With a great deal of fanfare, have a puppet reveal a card and then prompt students to identify the word. Continue in the same way, alternating puppets for each remaining card.

Building fluency:

Give Drew and Sue theatrical flair by having youngsters act out the story! Familiarize students with the story. As the class reads the booklet aloud, encourage a boy and a girl to act out the events using simple props.

Featured

High-Frequency Words

he	but
is	they
she	are
not	

Booklet Cover

Use with "Drew and Sue" on page 47.

Drew and Sue

Name _____

1

He is hungry. She is not.

2

He is sleepy. She is not.

3

He is quiet. She is not.

4

But they are both happy!

The Fair

Booklet Materials:

copy of pages 54–56 and the booklet
    page on page 57 for each student
scissors
crayons
stapler

Making the booklet:

1. Cut out the cover and booklet
   pages.
2. Stack the booklet pages in order
   behind the cover; then staple them
   together along the left-hand side.
3. Have the student write her name
   on the cover.
4. Have her color the pictures on the
   cover and booklet pages.

Introducing the featured words:

Introduce the words listed by writing them on the board and
discussing them. Or, if desired, introduce the words with this kid-
pleasing idea! Use the pattern on page 57 to make 11 construction paper ice-cream scoops. Write a different high-frequency
word from the list on each scoop. Also make a large brown
construction paper cone. Tape the cone to the bottom of a sheet
of chart paper and display it in your large-group area. Help
students identify the word on a scoop and then invite a youngster to tape it above the cone. Continue in the same way with
each remaining scoop until youngsters have made a towering
11-scoop treat. Then enjoy the booklet together.

Building fluency:

When youngsters have read through the booklet several times,
ask them to name the different kinds of foods the children ate at
the fair. When students reveal that the children ate candy, give
each youngster a Safe-T-Pop lollipop or lollipop cutout. Invite
each student to hold the lollipop by the wrapped end and use
it to follow the text as she rereads the booklet. If desired, have
students locate specific words on each page, using their lollipops
as pointers. When you are finished, invite each student to eat her
treat!

Featured
High-Frequency Words

we	but
went	do
to	not
the	very
were	now
so	

The Fair

Name _____

©The Mailbox® • *High-Frequency Word Booklets* • TEC60912

We went to the fair.

1

We ate ice cream.

2

We ate cookies.

3

Booklet Pages 4 and 5
Use with "The Fair" on page 53.

We ate candy.

4

We were so happy!

5

But we do not feel very good now.

6

Ice-Cream Scoop Pattern
Use with "Introducing the Featured Words" on page 53.

The Pig and the Cow

The Pig and the Cow

Name _____ James

The pig and the cow had tea.

Booklet Materials:

copy of pages 59–64 for each student
copy of page 65
crayons
scissors
stapler

Making the booklet:

1. Cut out the cover and booklet pages.
2. Stack the booklet pages in order; then staple them along the left side.
3. Have the student write his name on the cover.
4. Have him color the pictures on the cover and booklet pages.

Introducing the featured words:

Introduce the words listed by writing them on the board and discussing them. Or, if desired, introduce the words with the help of some farm friends! To do this, write each word on a separate card. Glue a pig or cow cutout (patterns on page 65) to each card. Then place the cards blank side out on your chalk tray. Have a child select a cutout and turn it around to reveal the word. Help him identify the word and then display it for the class. Continue in this manner with different students until all the words have been identified. Then enjoy the booklet together.

Building fluency:

When students have read through the booklet several times, give them additional practice with this partner center. Cut out the patterns on page 65 and prepare them for flannelboard use. Have each pair of students take a turn at the center. Invite one child to read the booklet aloud while his partner places the appropriate pieces on the flannelboard. Then have the partners switch roles.

Featured
High-Frequency Words

the	saw
and	a
went	made
to	when
had	

The Pig and the Cow

Name _____

The pig and the cow went to sea.

2

The pig and the cow had tea.

They saw a fish,

3

and they made a wish

4

when the pig and the cow went to sea.

5

pig

boat

star

tea set

cow

water

fish

What Did She Get?

Booklet Materials:

copy of pages 67–70 and the booklet page on
   page 71 for each student
copy of page 72
crayons
scissors
stapler
2 pipe cleaner halves for each student
tape

Making the booklet:

1. Cut out the cover and booklet pages.
2. Stack the booklet pages in order behind the cover; then staple them together along the left-hand side.
3. Have the student write her name on the cover.
4. Have her color the pictures on the cover and booklet pages.
5. Help her bend each pipe cleaner half into an arch. Then help her tape one pipe cleaner to the back of the booklet cover and one to the back of the last page to resemble shopping bag handles.

Introducing the featured words:

Introduce the words listed by writing them on the board and discussing them. Or, if desired, ask for a price check to introduce the words! To do this, make ten copies of the price tag pattern (page 71) on white construction paper. Cut out the tags and program each with a different featured high-frequency word. Arrange the tags on your chalk tray. Have a child select a tag. Help her identify the word; then encourage the class to repeat it. Continue in this manner with different students until all the words have been identified. Then enjoy the booklet together.

Building fluency:

After students have read through the booklet several times, encourage further reading with the shopping item picture cards on page 72. Make copies of the picture cards, color them, and mount each on a different sheet of construction paper. Invite six children to stand in front of the group, holding the picture cards. Ask the rest of the class to read the booklet chorally. Have the children show the picture cards at the appropriate points in the story.

Featured

High-Frequency Words

has	got
been	some
at	a
the	now
she	no

What Did She Get?

Name _____

Jill has been at the store.

1

She got some shoes.

2

She got some socks.

3

She got some lamps.

4

She got some clocks.

5

She got some books.

6

She got a bunny.

7

Now she has no more money!

8

Price Tag Pattern
Use with "Introducing the Featured Words" on page 66.

Shopping Item Picture Cards

Use with "Building Fluency" on page 66.

What Could It Be?

Booklet Materials:

copy of pages 74–77 for each student
crayons
scissors
glue
stapler

Making the booklet:

1. Cut out the cover, booklet pages, and box lid pattern.
2. Stack the booklet pages in order behind the cover; then staple them together along the left-hand side. (Set aside the box lid pattern for student use.)
3. Have the student write his name on the cover.
4. Have him color the pictures on the cover and booklet pages 1–5.
5. After introducing the booklet and an initial reading, help him write the name of a desired item on the line on booklet page 6.
6. Have him draw a corresponding picture in the box; then glue one edge of the box lid pattern over the picture as indicated.

Introducing the featured words:

Introduce the words listed by writing them on the board and discussing them. Or, if desired, introduce the words with the help of a mystery box! To do this, place in a lidded box index cards that you have programmed with the featured high-frequency words. Have a child remove a card from the box. Help him identify the word; then display it for the class. Continue in this manner with different students until all the words have been identified. Then enjoy the booklet together.

Building fluency:

When students have read through the booklet several times, extend the fun with some real mystery boxes! Give each small group of students a lidded box. Have a child in each group secretly place a classroom item in the box. Then have the group read the booklet in unison, pausing to allow the child to reveal his item before reading the last page together, revising the ending to reflect the box's contents. Continue until each child in the group has had a turn.

Featured

High-Frequency Words

what	a
could	you
it	for
be	me
an	is

What Could It Be?

Name _____

What could be inside?

1

Could it be an apple?

2

Could it be a clock?

3

Could it be an umbrella?

4

Could you open it for me?

5

It is a _____.

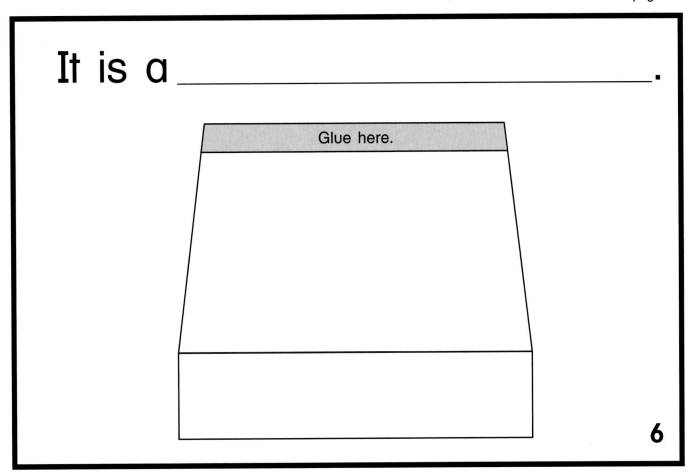

Glue here.

6

I Can!

Booklet Materials:

copy of pages 79–82 and the booklet
 page on page 83 for each student
crayons
scissors
stapler

Making the booklet:

1. Cut out the cover and booklet pages.
2. Stack the booklet pages in order behind the cover; then staple them together along the left-hand side.
3. Have the student write her name on the cover.
4. Have her color the pictures on the cover and booklet pages 1–7.
5. After introducing the booklet, have each child write and draw to complete page 8.

Introducing the featured words:

Introduce the words listed by writing them on the board and discussing them. Or, if desired, put the words in the spotlight! To do this, copy the words onto a chart and dim the lights. Have a child shine a flashlight on a word. Help her identify the word; then encourage the class to repeat it. Continue in this manner with different students until all the words have been identified. Then enjoy the booklet together.

Building fluency:

After students have read through the booklet several times, have them work in small groups. Encourage each group to read the first seven pages chorally. Invite each child to share her sentence and illustration from page eight with her group. Then award each child her very own "I Can!" badge (pattern on page 83).

Featured
High-Frequency Words

I	a
can	what
my	you
put	do
on	

1

I can

tie my shoes.

I Can!

Name _____

I can

swing high.

3

I can

use glue.

2

5

I can

write a letter.

4

I can

catch a firefly.

What can you you do?

7

I can

put on a sweater. 6

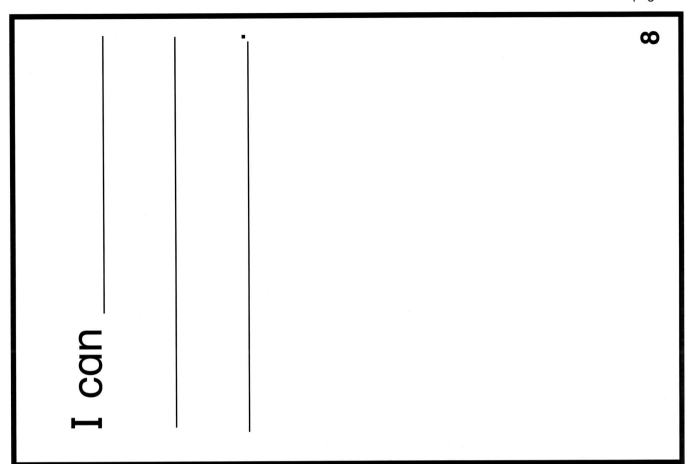

8

I can _____
_____
_____.

I can
read a book!

Ask me to read
it to you!

©The Mailbox®

I can
read a book!

Ask me to read
it to you!

©The Mailbox®

Max and Mom

Booklet Materials:

copy of pages 85–88 and the booklet page on page 89 for each student
crayons
scissors
stapler

Making the booklet:

1. Cut out the cover and booklet pages.
2. Stack the booklet pages in order behind the cover; then staple them together along the left-hand side.
3. Have the student write his name on the cover.
4. Have him color the pictures on the cover and booklet pages.

Introducing the featured words:

Introduce the high-frequency words listed by writing them on the board and discussing them. Or, if desired, make a bouquet of words! To do this, make seven copies of the flower patterns on page 89. Write each word on a different flower. Use removable adhesive to attach the flowers to a board, blank side out. Explain that the flowers represent a special surprise in the story you are about to read. Have a child choose a flower and turn it over. Help him identify the word; then encourage the class to repeat it. Continue in this manner with different students until all the words have been identified. Then enjoy the booklet together.

Building fluency:

After students have read through the booklet several times, provide your budding readers with a reason to read it once more! Give each child a small flower sticker to stick over his index fingernail. Have him run this finger flower under the words to track the print as he reads the booklet again.

Featured
High-Frequency Words

come	you
said	are
now	for
will	

Max and Mom

Name _____

"Come, Max," said Mom.

—

2

Max sat.

3

"Come now, Max," said Mom.

4

Max sat.

5

"Max, will you please come now," said Mom.

Booklet Pages 6 and 7

Use with "Max and Mom" on page 84.

6

Max came.

7

"These are for you," said Max.

Booklet Page 8
Use with "Max and Mom" on page 84.

Flower Patterns
Use with "Introducing the Featured Words" on page 84.

8

"Thank you, Max," said Mom.

Friends

Booklet Materials:

copy of pages 91–96 for each student
crayons
scissors
stapler

Making the booklet:

1. Cut out the cover and booklet pages.
2. Stack the booklet pages in order behind the cover; then staple them together along the left-hand side.
3. Have the student write her name on the cover.
4. Have her color the pictures on the cover and booklet pages.

Introducing the booklet:

Introduce the words listed by writing them on the board and discussing them. Or, if desired, combine the word introduction with a secret code that shares the booklet's theme! To do this, write each high-frequency word on a separate index card in black ink. Turn the cards over. Then use a red pen to write one letter (including the exclamation point) on the back of each card to spell the message "It is about pals. Then arrange the cards in your chalk tray so that the high-frequency words show and the message is in order. Have a student select a word; then help her identify it. As each word is identified, turn it over to reveal the secret letter. Continue in the same manner with different students until all the words have been identified and the message is revealed. Read the message and then turn the cards over so the high-frequency words are displayed. Then enjoy the booklet together.

Building fluency:

After students have read through the booklet several times, have them work in small groups. Have two students in each group play the parts of the girl and the mouse to dramatize the story while the others read the booklet text chorally. Repeat the activity until each child in the group has had a turn to play a part.

Featured

High-Frequency Words

my	we
in	like
a	to
big	and
house	all
is	day
little	I

Friends

Name _____

©The Mailbox® • *High-Frequency Word Booklets* • TEC60912

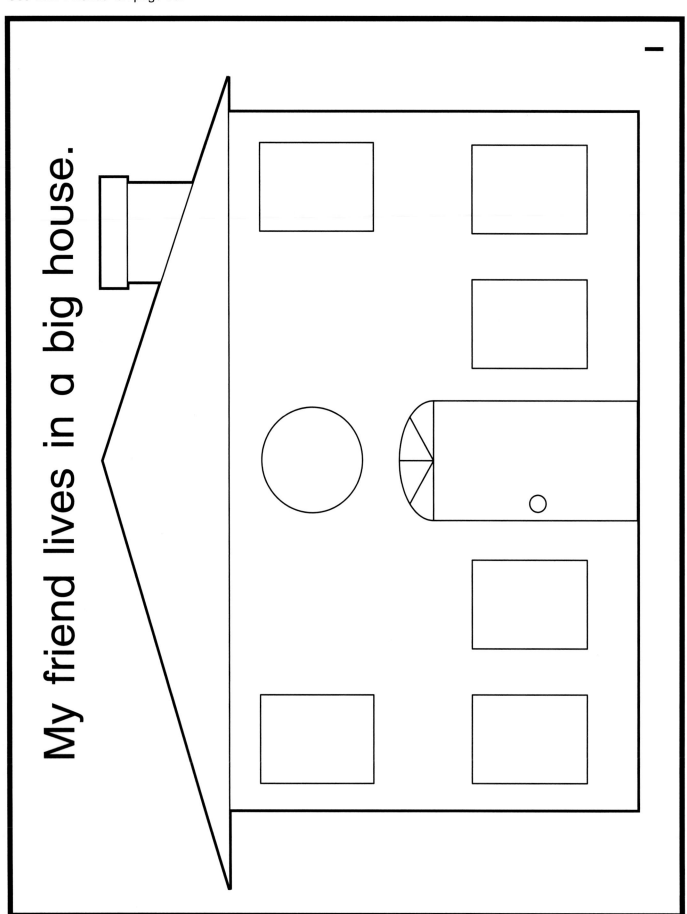

My friend lives in a big house.

2

My friend is a little mouse.

3

We like to run and play.

We like to sing all day.

4

5

I like my friend a lot!